A life well lived is about small little acts of LOVE.

Dubbed the "The Little Lemonpreneur," Vivienne Harr, applied the only business know-how she had and in less than one year, along with the help of her family, started her own lemonade company.

And as you will see, the results have been amazing.

In this book, Vivienne tells her story about what inspired her, how it all came together, and what you should do next time someone tells you "No!"

Make a Stand!

We are excited to welcome Vivienne as our Edgemaker ambassador, empowering kids all over the world to share their stories and make their stand.

Please join Vivienne on her mission and help us spread LOVE like chocolate sauce all over the world...

Sincerely,
Chocolate Sauce

Shelley Lewis
Publisher, Chocolate Sauce

Enriching children both Big and Small

Help us turn the leaf and end child slavery...

Make a Stand

When life gives you lemons, change the world!

Created by Vivienne Harr (age 9)
(with the help of Turner, age 3)

Illustrated by Alexandra Harr
Graphic Design by Dunja Pantic

by
chocolate
sauce

Hiya everyone!
My name is Vivienne.
I am 9 years old and
this is my brother Turner.

I am ending child slavery in my lifetime.
Would you like to hear my story?

One day, I saw a photo of two boys with rocks strapped on their heads.

I learned they were slaves.

I thought slavery ended with Abraham Lincoln, but I was wrong about that.

Best ever made
Lemon - aid

Kids should be Free!

Lemonade was the only business experience I had. So I set up my

lemonade stand

(only not your ordinary lemonade stand).

I said I would set up my stand every day, come rain or shine, until I raised $100,000 to free children from slavery.

My mom said,
"Honey, that's a lot of
lemonade!"

I said,
"If I set my heart to it,
it can work."

So, I did!

We got a special recipe from Nonnie and Grandpa, who have been making lemonade for like, hundreds of years!

We went shopping for fair-trade ingredients. That means people were treated fairly to get those ingredients.

Seems fair to me!

To reach my goal we would have to make the best-ever-made lemon - aid.

And that's just what we did!

We made the lemonade and put everything (including my dog, Buddy) in our wagon and went to the park.

Kenneth "Doc" Edgar Park

(the same park where my papa played when he was my age).

I had no idea what would happen next.

On our first day,
we had balloons
and lots of fun
but not everybody
stopped by.

My papa said,
"You don't need everyone.
You don't need most.
You just need enough."

Most days it felt great making a stand.

Some days, it didn't feel great making a stand.

(But I did it anyway.)

Every day my family was there supporting me.
When you have that, you can do anything.

Even Turner made a stand
with me. Everyday!

I used to call him "Turnado"
because he would wreck things.
But, now I call him

"my Make a Stand Man!"

FREE Lemonade

Around day twenty, we started doing better. I learned how to count money. I opened my own bank account.

"Look at all those nickels!"

All along we were charging $2 a cup. It would take, like, hundreds of years at that price!

Pay What's In Your Heart.

So on Day 34, I started saying: "Pay what's in your heart."

This Lemonade is not for sale because Kids are not for sale in other words its FREE

The dollars started going up and up and up!
One man gave $120 for a cup.
He said:
"My wallet is empty, but my heart is full."

One day, a nice man talked about my story in the news.

Things got busy busy busy after that.

Lots of news started coming and coming. I must have told my story a billion times. It was fun doing that!

They flew me to a big tv show to make a stand and sent
a long car!
I was on a big stage with big lights. Up there I said,
"Gandhi was one person, Mother Theresa was one
person, Martin Luther King was one person.
Why can't you be one person who helps?"
The audience stood up and cheered. For a long time.
Like, a really long time.

People treated me differently, but I was no different.

Just me

I was just following my heart and doing my part.

My mom and dad said when you do good, it comes back to you.

I found that is really true!

MAKE A STAND
Vivienne Harr

November 2nd. 2012

Pay to the order of NOT FOR SALE $ 30,000-

memo Hope and Freedom   Vivienne Harr

THE 2012 NOT FOR SALE

GLOBAL
FORUM

JUSTICE FOR THE BOTTOM BILLION
Where the movement gathers to bring about social
change and an end to modern-day slavery.

Vivienne
Harr

juniper

Then I was invited to
the "Global Forum"
where people
who change the world go.

Then it
happened.
I met Lisa
Kristine!
Remember,
the one who
took the
photo
of the two
boys with
the rocks
strapped on
their heads?

I asked her about those boys.
She said they live hard lives,
and that I was helping them
a lot. Then she gave me a big
hug. That kept me going, I tell ya!

I even met a famous
baseball player named
Jeremy Affeldt. He had just
won the World Series!
He said,
"You have a strong heart.
You are my hero."

His hero?
He was 11 feet tall!

I heard a hurricane had hit New York City.

I wanted to make a stand by singing in Times Square.

I gave half of my money to New York and half of my money to child slavery.

Both of those things are making a stand, because both matter to my heart.

I sang "Firework" by Katy Perry. People cheered and cried (my dad mostly, but don't tell him I told you).

TODAY ONLY
MATINEE
THE LITTLE LEMON
IN THE BIG APPLE

After my song, a tv person asked me, "If you only had one day to live, what would you do?"
I said, "This."

After 173 days of making
a stand in a row,
on a cold New York day,
would you believe it?
I did it. I reached my goal.

$101,320 to end
child slavery!

The next day, my parents said:
"You did it, Honey.
You're done!"
I said,
"Is child slavery done?"
They shook their heads.
I said,
"Then I am not done."

They said:
"Honey, ending
child slavery
might not be
possible."
I said,
"Why not?"

I thought :
What if I bottled up
my lemon-aid?
What if everyone bought it?
Could we end child slavery
that way?

Like always, my parents made a stand with me.
They helped me figure out how to
bottle the hope.

So we did!

It works like this :

1. I give you lemon-aid.
2. You give what's in your heart.
3. We give kids freedom.

I came up with a new word for my business :

A "giveness"

A business takes. A giveness gives.

People liked that. And Make A Stand got bigger.

My mom said,

"Honey, your moment is becoming a movement."

Then I appeared on stage at Wisdom 2.0!

Make a Stand became more when we went to Moore
(Oklahoma) to help people from the tornadoes.
Make a Stand means making a stand for what you believe in.
For what's in front of you. For what's in your heart.

It's funny.
Along the way,
some people said:
"You are too little.
You can't make a
difference?"
I said:
"Why not?"

Some people said:
"You're only 9.
You can't start
your own lemonade
company."
I said:
"Why not?"

Some people said:
"You can't have
a lemonade stand
every single day."
I said:
"Why not?"

Some people said:
"You're helping victims
of child slavery.
You can't help victims
of tornadoes."
I said:
"Why not?"

Making a Stand is about finding what's in your heart and doing something about it. When people say you can't, don't worry. JUST SAY WHAT I SAY:

"Why not? I will Make a Stand!"

Now you know my story. I'd like to know yours!

What do you stand for?

What will you do?
(You can write it down right here.)

I _____

pledge to
Make A Stand to:

Great!
Now, do it.

Make a Stand!

I know you'll do great!

Biya!

Vivienne Harr!

Make A Stand didn't start as a product. It started as a *promise*— deep in the heart of a little girl who wanted to make the world a better place.

As this social purpose company grows, our unwavering fidelity is to Miss Vivienne's original vision: to end child slavery. That is our true North. Vivienne believes that anything is possible, and that authentic belief is pulling us over seemingly-impossible obstacles.

You see, kids don't think of the reasons why they can't do something; they just do it. We grown-ups can learn from that. And, if we're willing to embrace the "magic of the child," extraordinary things can happen.

Make A Stand is a moment that became a movement, because people like you have stood with Vivienne.

On behalf of the Make A Stand family, and our family, we extend our heartfelt gratitude to you for standing with Vivienne and buying this book. Please share our story with those you love, and— make a stand for what you believe in.

Let that magic fill your sails on the beautiful journey of life.

~Eric Harr, Founder & CEO, Make a Stand, Inc. -- and most importantly, Vivienne's dad.

To the children living in slavery. Don't ever give up hope. We're coming for you.

Alone we can do so little. Together we can do so much." ~Helen Keller

Those words encapsulate the Make a Stand movement. Without the efforts of thousands of people, Make a Stand's moment cannot become a movement.

When Vivienne set up her stand on our street-corner, nobody knew about it. When the news broke, everybody knew about it. Thousands of people from every corner of the globe stood with her. So, we start our acknowledgements there: Thank you for standing with Vivienne.

To: Tony, Gary, Jenny, the Make a Stand Team, Steph, our investors who took great leaps of faith, Daphne, Lisa, Shelley, Katie and the Fair Trade family, our friends at Stillmotion (Patrick, Grant, David, Jeremy, Joyce and the team), our Twitter family (Jack, Biz, Evan, Dick, Mike, Gabriel and the team), Libby, John, Turner, Vivienne, and finally – TO YOU!

We Love You!

Please visit

www.makeastand.com/book

and see!